A

CHRISTMAS

PARABLE

A Christmas
PARABLE

SECOND EDITION

BOYD K. PACKER
ILLUSTRATED BY THE AUTHOR

EAGLE
GATE

SALT LAKE CITY, UTAH

Only Standard Works, official statements, and other
publications written under assignment from the First
Presidency and Council of the Twelve Apostles are
considered authorized publications by The Church of
Jesus Christ of Latter-day Saints. Other
publications, including this one,
are the responsibility of the writer.

The Author

ISBN 0-88494-901-X

Printed in the United States of America
Publishers Press, Salt Lake City, UT

10   9   8   7   6   5   4   72082-2802

A parable is "a brief, simple story told to illustrate or teach a moral or spiritual truth." This is a Christmas parable.

$\mathcal{H}$e was a natural-born family man. He had *wanted* to get married, and he found the perfect girl who had wanted to be a farmer's

wife. They wanted children. And they
made the most of family life, and of
Christmas.

This winter day he worked in
the shed trying to salvage parts
from a broken mower. He
thought of Christmas
and he was worried.

Christmas bothered him. And
it bothered him that Christmas
bothered him. Christmas was home
and family and fireplaces and happy
times with presents and good meals
and memories of better times.
Christmas symbolized things that
mattered most to him.

This had not been a good year; the crops had been poor, and there was the accident.

If only he had not been in a cast for those weeks! His boys had done the best they could, but they were only boys.

The mower had broken down. He could not afford the new parts, so he had wired it together. Because of that, it was damaged beyond repair. Had it not been for the kindness of a neighbor who loaned him a mower, his hay would not have been harvested at all. By that time the hay was way past prime and did not bring a good price.

There had been hard times on the farm before, but not three years in a row. The previous night he had gone over the books with his wife. Another year like this and they would lose the farm.

Perhaps they could make presents for the little ones. The older ones in school would not expect more than the clothes they should have had to begin the school year. But he didn't know how he and his wife could do even that much.

It bothered him greatly. For the first time in his life he wished Christmas would not come. Why could they not hurry on to January, and then spring would come and bring hope of a better season.

At that moment his wife called, "Come wash up for supper!"

After supper the two of them talked until a late hour. They talked about Christmas.

They also talked of the reunion scheduled for later that month.

This reunion was very important to both of them. Weeks earlier she had casually asked him which dress she should wear. He understood, and he insisted, even commanded, that she get a new one, even if he had to sell the best milk cow to do it. It would be her Christmas present. Whatever else happened, he was determined that she would be dressed as well as the others.

She finally bowed to his insistence and bought a modestly priced dress.

She had looked so lovely when she modeled it for him that memories of honeymoon days had captivated them both.

Now, as they talked things over this evening, each tried to encourage the other. But both were worried. For the first time they were losing hope.

He slept fitfully at first. Finally "bone-

tired weariness," which is the best of all sedatives, took effect. He dropped into a deep sleep. Presently he began to dream.

His dream was a reenactment of the evening before. He found himself back in the shed stripping parts from the broken mower. His wife called, "Come wash up for supper!" just as she had before. He went toward the house just as he had done before.

In this dream, he went to the sink in the back hallway to wash up, just as he always did. And then it happened! For some reason, the dirt would not come off.

At first he thought the water was too cold, or it was a poor soap. He briskly rubbed the soap into suds, but the dirt did not come off. He reached for a cloth and scrubbed his hands. The stains did not yield. What was the matter with him?

He held his hands up and looked closely. He noticed around his fingernails little specks of red paint, just the color of the barn. But it was twelve years since he had painted the barn. All traces of the paint had been washed from his hands years ago. In fact, the barn needed painting again.

He noticed other stains and recognized some of them. There were faint odors of chemicals and animal smells and grease from the

farm machinery. As he looked at his hands each stain in turn seemed to emerge from the others. His memory was quickened and he remembered when each had been put there—and he remembered washing each one away.

He had never been afraid to dirty his hands with honest work, for that is the lot of the farmer; but he had a certain pride in being well groomed. From the days of his courtship he had been meticulously clean and had always kept his hair neatly trimmed. He was fussy about having clothes that fit properly. His wife admired that and quite willingly kept them cleaned and pressed.

But why were those stains on his hands;

layer upon layer of them? Why would they
not wash away? Some were barely visible, but
they were there—all of them.

He splashed about, fighting to get the stains off. He dipped his arms into the sink to the elbow, sleeves and all. To his surprise, the dirt drained from the sleeves and they were clean, but not his hands! He rolled up the wet sleeves and looked at his arms. They were the same as his hands, stained with every spot that was ever put there.

It was then that he turned to the mirror and slumped over in despair. It was as though he had not washed in years.

Into his mind came thoughts of the

reunion, the homecoming, and he grew sick. He could not even go to supper, much less attend the reunion, covered with a lifetime of dirt.

Then, as can happen in a dream, he was caught in a swirl of humiliation and futility. He was pulled apart by opposing forces of misery and fear.

For the first time in his life he experienced *absolute despair!*

All at once, abruptly, he awakened. Thank God it was a dream! Only a dream! He felt his face. It was clean. He rubbed his hands; they were rough and chapped, but they were clean. He lay awake brooding for what seemed like hours, till eventually that sedative, exhaustion, took effect again and he slept.

Morning came, and he arose as usual when the rooster crowed. (Actually it was the light in the kitchen window that stirred the rooster to his first call of the morning.) He roused the boys and they went to do the chores in the usual way.

As is often the case when dreams have great meaning, this dream was not on his mind when first he awakened. He had not forgotten it; it just was

Peace
Be unto this House

not present in his mind. Dreams of this kind
come back and are relived during the day.

Not until she called him to wash up for
breakfast and he stood at the sink did it all
come back to him.

He washed his hands and the dirt came off. He looked in the mirror and his face was clean. But he paused for a long moment in deep thought. The dream meant something. But what?

He was not really a sentimental man but he had deep feelings about his family and about farming. Something happened inside his soul when new life appeared each spring. And when growing things responded to his care he had tender, even spiritual, feelings. In his own silent way he was a praying man. He had offered constant prayers of late. It was this spiritual part of his nature which responded so readily to Christmas. That is why Christmas this year bothered him, and why he was bothered that it bothered him.

At breakfast, his wife noticed

that he was troubled. But worried looks were not unusual these days. Nevertheless she asked if anything had disturbed him. He turned his head a little in a gesture which meant neither yes nor no.

Then she reminded him it was Sunday. As usual, he encouraged her to take the children to church. And, as usual, he expected to putter around the farm trying to catch up on work that was never quite done.

There had been very little of church in his growing up. He had been baptized, and that was about all. It was amazing, in a way, that he came out such a decent, steady man. He wanted his children to attend

church with their mother.
But lately the older boys
wanted to stay with
him.

This Sunday
his wife urged
him to come
along. The
children were
not on the
program, it was not
Christmas or Easter–just
an ordinary Sunday. But
today he *must* come! It would help him, she
was sure of it. "Please," she pleaded, "come
this once." It was always hard for him to

resist his wife when she said please. And so it was that the whole family went to church.

He sat uncomfortably with her in the Gospel Doctrine class. The struggling teacher had only modest teaching ability. The lesson was on baptism, but he was not interested in that. His mind was on the disturbing dream of the night before.

He could hear the teacher reading a scripture. Though he was not really listening, two words hit him with great force. The words were *washed clean*.

He startled his wife by asking the teacher to read the scripture again. It was his first-ever response in a Sunday School class.

The teacher read again:

And after they have paid the penalty of their transgressions, and are *washed clean*, [they] shall receive a reward according to their works, for they are heirs of salvation (D&C 138:59).

The teacher asked if he had another
question, but he simply shook his head. He
was too choked to speak. He had felt
something!

What he felt was the exact opposite to the dark, suffocating despair in his dream. It was not a new feeling exactly. He had felt it before, but never in this intensity.

It was akin to the feeling he had about family and farming. He felt it when his children were born. He felt it, or something like it, when growing things responded to his care. And *always* he felt it at Christmas. It was this that made Christmas so appealing to him. It had been subtle and fleeting before, but now it came with overwhelming power.

He listened intently to that unskilled teacher. When one of the class members was asked to define baptism, she said it was an ordinance to wash away our sins.

Now a class member read another scripture:

Now I say unto you that ye must repent, and be born again; for the Spirit saith if ye are not born again ye cannot inherit the kingdom of heaven; therefore come and be baptized unto repentance,

that ye may be *washed* from your sins, that ye
may have faith on the Lamb of God, who
taketh away the sins of the world, who is
mighty to save and to *cleanse* from all
unrighteousness (Alma 7:14).

Again the words struck him with force: *washed . . . sins . . . baptism . . . cleanse from all unrighteousness.*

The word *Christmas* was not used in the lesson, but the word *gift* was. The teacher read from the New Testament:

> Then Peter said . . . , Repent, and be baptized every one of you in the name of Jesus Christ for the remission of sins, and ye shall receive the *gift* of the Holy Ghost (Acts 2:38).

That ordinary, unskilled teacher closed her scriptures and gave a sigh of relief. The lessons were always a struggle for her.

On the way home her husband asked how the class had gone. She thought she had not done very well. But one member had brought her husband. He had never attended before, and he had seemed to be deeply moved by the lesson.

She did not know that the lesson on *baptism* had been for him a lesson on *Christmas*.

In the days that followed, his mind kept returning to his dream and to the Sunday School lesson. Only a day or two after that lesson he read on a Christmas card:

Behold, the angel of the Lord appeared unto him in a dream, saying, Joseph, thou son of David, fear not to take unto thee

Mary thy wife: for that which is conceived in her is of the Holy Ghost. And she shall bring forth a son, and thou shalt call his name Jesus: for he shall save his people from their sins. (Matthew 1:20–21.)

For the first time he understood! He knew what that meant.

He was a man with little-boy feelings about Christmas. The birth of the Christ had always been more or less present for him in that season. But now the symbols of Christmas which he loved had real meaning. Gifts from the wise men now represented something, as did the tree and the star. But now, the promise of redemption had entered

the scene. He had lost nothing from the
appealing traditions of Christmas; in fact,
they now had greater meaning.

He understood! For the first time he understood what the gift was!

The problems of life were not lessened by his new understanding, but there was a new power working within him. The problems remained, but the troubled heart did not. He had new kinds of conversations with his wife. On Sunday she no longer needed to say please.

They attended that important reunion dressed in the best they had; modest, well groomed, and very clean.

After the reunion, for the first time he told his wife of the dream. They talked into the night of what it meant. Now he understood that, just as he could wash up for supper, there was a way to become spiritually clean. Because of the

first Christmas and what followed it, he could get clean and he could stay clean.

They talked of another reunion awaiting them beyond the veil. To enter there one must be clean, spiritually clean. He listened as his wife explained the Atonement and the Resurrection. He understood! For the first time, he understood! Because of that first

Christmas, they would live eternally. They could enter in and be together there—a family. This was the gift!

No wonder choirs of angels sang. No wonder signs appeared in the heavens. No wonder shepherds and kings learned to follow stars.

He quietly said the words *washed* and *clean* and *Christmas* over again, and his heart was filled with joy.

"You know," he said, "it is as though each of us is given a precious gift wrapped in scenes of home and family and holly and trees and traditions. It is so beautiful on the

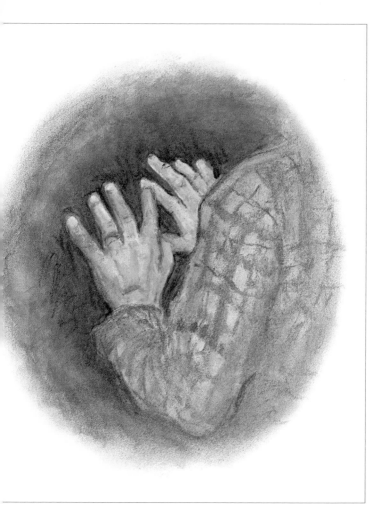

 outside that we
never really open
it.

"Only when the
wrapping wears through with age, or troubled
times press in upon us, or a family scene is
torn apart, will we open the gift. We then find
that all that is pictured on the wrapping that
we love so much is not lost; it is all there
inside."

"Yes," she said, "it seems that only when
the fabric of life is torn will we look inside of
ourselves; there to find who we are, who *he* is,
and what gift he offers us. Then each may
follow his own star to Bethlehem and kneel
there to worship."

So ends a Christmas parable. I have opened that gift and have seen inside; I have heard his voice and received a witness, even a special witness of him. I

pray God that each of us this Christmas will at last open the gift and discover who *we* are, and who *he* is. Then we will know what Christmas means and what the Gift is. This is my Christmas prayer for all of us.

Washed Clean

A Poem

*I*n ancient times the cry "Unclean!"
Would warn of lepers near.
   "Unclean! Unclean!" the words rang out;
Then all drew back in fear,

*L*est by the touch of lepers' hands
They, too, would lepers be.
   There was no cure in ancient times,
Just hopeless agony.

*N*o soap, no balm, no medicine
Could stay disease or pain.
   There was no salve, no cleansing bath
To make them well again.

*B*ut there was One, the record shows,
Whose touch could make them pure;
   Could ease their awful suffering,
Their rotting flesh restore.

*H*is coming long had been foretold.

Signs would precede His birth.

A Son of God to woman born,

With power to cleanse the earth.

*T*he day He made ten lepers whole,

The day He made them clean,[1]

Well symbolized His ministry

And what His life would mean.

*H*owever great that miracle,
This was not why He came.
He came to rescue every soul
From death, from sin, from shame.

*F*or greater miracles, He said,
His servants yet would do,[2]
To rescue every living soul,
Not just heal up the few.

*T*hough we're redeemed from mortal death,
We still can't enter in
  Unless we're clean, cleansed every whit,
From every mortal sin.

*W*hat must be done to make us clean,
We cannot do alone.
  The law, to be a law, requires
A pure one must atone.

*H*e taught that justice will be stayed

Till mercy's claim be heard

　If we repent and are baptized

And live by every word.

*T*hat is the never-ending gift

That came that Christmas day

　When Mary first held close her son

And shepherds came to pray.

If we could only understand

All we have heard and seen,

We'd know there is no greater gift

Than those two words—"Washed clean!"

Boyd K. Packer

1. Luke 17:12.
2. John 14:12.

Christmas Memories

Christmas Memories

Christmas Memories

ISBN 0-88494-901-X

EAN

51395

9 780884 949015

SKU 2883963 U.S. $13.95